Cup of Grace

CHERIE RICKARD RN, CG-C

Copyright © 2025 Cherie Rickard RN, CG-C

Publisher: Empowerment is Beauty

All rights reserved.

ISBN: 978-0-9992267-2-8

FOREWARD

Imagine waking up each day with a renewed sense of hope, like a fresh breath of life washing over you.

That's the invitation behind Cup of Grace, a 30-day devotional that doesn't just offer words on a page—it offers an experience.

An experience with God Himself, not just a routine or a ritual, but a real encounter with His love, guidance, and purpose for your life.

This book isn't about religion; it's about relationship. The Bible tells us that real transformation begins with renewing our minds (Romans 12:2).

In Cup of Grace, Cherie gently leads you on a journey to do just that—inviting you each day to set aside the noise, soak in God's Word, and let His truth reshape your thoughts, bringing fresh hope, strength, and purpose to your life.

Cherie, the heart behind this book, is a woman who knows what it's like to face life's hardest trials. She has walked through darkness, yet through it all, she has held on to her unshakable faith in God.

Her story is one of resilience and courage, and for anyone who hears it, it's a powerful reminder that there's strength and peace waiting for you too—even when life takes an unexpected turn.

In Cup of Grace, Cherie welcomes you to begin each day with two essentials: time with God and, for many of us, a comforting cup of coffee. Each entry in this devotional is filled with Scripture, reflections, heartfelt prayers, and affirmations that remind you of God's grace, provision, power, and His plan to bring peace and strength into your life.

Imagine the next 30 days as an invitation—a chance to step closer to the One who knows you better than you know yourself. This isn't about a to-do list or just getting through another devotional; it's about connecting with God's love in a way that fills you, lifts you, and changes you from the inside out.

My prayer is that Cup of Grace becomes a part of your daily rhythm, drawing you closer to the One who provides all you need. Whether you're in a season of joy or facing life's struggles, may you find comfort, strength, and peace in these pages—and may this journey be one you look forward to each morning with your yummy cup of coffee, knowing that God Himself is waiting to meet you there.

Nicole Wood

Solution-Based Counselor, Bestselling Author of Breakthrough Prayers & Declarations, and Co-Founder of PrayerFountain.com

CONTENTS

Guided By Grace 8
Live in Abundance................................ 12
Delight and Trust 16
Creating a Pure Heart 20
Peace over Anxiety 24
God is Your Shield................................28
Stand Firm in Faith...............................32
God's Higher Ways...............................36
Love in Action......................................40
Never Alone 44
Light for Your Path 48
Wisdom from Above 52
Walk in Obedience...............................56
Power of Forgiveness..........................60
Give and Receive 64
Soul Fully Satisfied..............................68
Blessings Without Sorrow 72
Prosper and Thrive..............................76

Honor Your Temple 80
God Grants Desires 84
Delight and Trust 88
Confidence Brings Reward 92
Write the Vision 96
Grace is Enough 100
Run with Endurance 104
Be Strong, Stand 108
Honor and Overflow 112
Believe it's Possible 116
Release the Burden 120
God Sees You 124

To My Family,

Your love, prayers, and unwavering support mean the world to me. Whether it's a simple word of encouragement when I need it most or just sitting with me in the quiet moments, I feel your presence lifting me up.

Your belief in this journey God has called me to strengthens me, even on my hardest days.

Every prayer and every kind word fuel me in ways you may never fully realize.

Thank you for being my rock, my safe place, and my biggest blessing. I'm beyond grateful for each of you—today and always.

Love you all!

DAY 1:

Guided By Grace

Scripture: Psalm 23:1 (NIV)
"The Lord is my shepherd, I lack nothing."

Reflection:
In a world filled with constant demands, it's easy to feel overwhelmed or like we're missing something. But this verse reminds us that with God as our Shepherd, we lack nothing.

Application:
When you feel anxious or unsure about what lies ahead, remember that God is already leading the way. Instead of focusing on what you don't have, focus on the abundance God has already given you. Trust that He will provide for every need in His perfect timing.

1. **Trust in God's Provision** – Stop worrying about what you lack and remind yourself that God will always provide what you need.
2. **Follow His Guidance** – Just like sheep trust their shepherd, lean on God's direction in your decisions, big and small.
3. **Live with Contentment** – Instead of focusing on what you don't have, practice gratitude for the ways God is already providing for you.

Prayer:
"Lord, thank You for being my Shepherd, guiding me, and meeting every need in my life. Help me to rest in Your provision and trust that I truly lack nothing when You are with me. In Jesus' name, amen."

Affirmation:
"I have all that I need in Christ, and I trust God's perfect provision in every area of my life."

Inspiration for the Day:
Today, trust that you lack nothing.

Wherever God leads, He provides. Rest in His peace and know that He is already taking care of what concerns you.

www..queenbeetransformation.com

Reflection of the day

Day 2:

Live in Abundance

Scripture: John 10:10b (NIV)
"I came that they may have life and have it abundantly."

Reflection:
Jesus promises not just life, but life in abundance. This means more than just surviving or getting by; it's a life filled with purpose, joy, and spiritual richness. Through Christ, we are given access to a life that's full of His peace, grace, and love.

Application:
Think about areas of your life where you feel like you're just getting by. How can you invite Jesus to bring abundance into those areas? Embrace His promise by

seeking fullness in your relationship with Him and others, and by living in gratitude.

1. **Embrace God's Best** – Stop settling for a life of fear, doubt, or lack—God wants you to thrive!
2. **Align Your Life with His Will** – Choose daily actions that reflect a life filled with His joy, peace, and purpose.
3. **Reject the Enemy's Lies** – The enemy wants to steal your joy—combat negativity with faith and scripture.

Prayer:
"Dear Jesus, thank You for offering me abundant life. Help me to walk in Your fullness and to experience the richness of life through Your grace, love, and peace. Lead me in living each day with purpose and joy. Amen."

Affirmation:
"I live in the abundance of Christ, experiencing a life full of purpose, grace, and joy."

Inspiration for the Day:
Live with an abundant mindset today. Let Christ's fullness fill your life with joy, gratitude, and purpose as you go about your day.

www..queenbeetransformation.com

Reflection of the day

Day 3:

Delight and Trust

Scripture: Psalm 37:4-5 (KJV)
"Delight thyself also in the Lord; and he shall give thee desires of thine heart. Commit thy way unto the Lord; trust also in him; and he shall bring it to pass."

Reflection:
When we find joy and delight in God, our desires start to align with His will. He shapes our hearts and brings His perfect plans to life when we commit our ways to Him. Trust God to take control, knowing that He works all things for good.

Application:
Evaluate the desires of your heart. Are they aligned with God's will? As you delight in

Him today, commit your dreams and plans to His care, trusting that He will guide and fulfill them according to His perfect timing.

1. **Seek God First** – Make your relationship with Him your top priority, and your desires will align with His.
2. **Surrender Your Plans** – Trust that when you release control, He guides you toward your best future.
3. **Stay Expectant** – Live with confidence that God will fulfill His promises in the right time.

Prayer:
"Lord, I delight in You and trust that You know the deepest desires of my heart. I commit my plans to You, knowing that You will bring to pass what aligns with Your will. Help me to trust in Your timing and ways. Amen."

Affirmation:
"My desires align with God's will, and I trust Him to bring His plans for my life to fulfillment."

Inspiration for the Day:
Take joy in God today, knowing that as you delight in Him, He is shaping your desires and bringing them to life in His perfect timing.

www..queenbeetransformation.com

Reflection of the day

Day 4:

Creating a Pure Heart

Scripture: Psalm 51:10 (NIV)
"Create in me a clean heart, O God; and renew a right spirit within me."

Reflection:
A clean heart is essential for a vibrant relationship with God. When we invite Him to renew our spirits, He transforms us from within leading to spiritual growth and intimacy with Him.

Application:
Spend a few moments in silence, asking God to reveal any areas of your heart that need cleansing. Make a conscious effort to live in a way that reflects His love and grace.

1. **Daily Heart Check** – Ask God to reveal anything in your heart that needs cleansing and healing.
2. **Stay in His Word** – Regularly reading scripture renews and strengthens your spirit.
3. **Live in Repentance** – Don't hold onto guilt—seek God's forgiveness and move forward in grace.

Prayer:
"Lord, I ask You to cleanse my heart and renew my spirit. Help me to live in a way that honors You and reflects Your love. Thank You for Your mercy and grace. Amen."

Affirmation:
"I am being transformed by God's love, and my heart is renewed and made clean through His grace."

Inspiration for the Day:
Seek God's cleansing today. Allow His love to renew your heart and spirit, leading you into deeper intimacy with Him.

www..queenbeetransformation.com

Reflection of the day

Day 5:

Peace over Anxiety

Scripture: Psalm 94:19 (NIV)
"When my anxious thoughts multiply within me, Your comforts delight me."

Reflection:
Anxiety can overwhelm us, but in those moments, God's comfort is available. He understands our worries and brings peace to our hearts. By focusing on His presence, we can find joy and delight even amid chaos and uncertainty.

Application:
Identify any anxious thoughts that are weighing you down today. Take a moment to turn those worries over to God, seeking His comfort and peace.

1. **Turn to God First** – When anxiety hits, go to Him in prayer instead of overthinking or worrying.
2. **Replace Fear with Praise** – Worship and gratitude shift your focus from stress to His goodness.
3. **Lean on His Comfort** – Remember that God's presence brings peace greater than any temporary relief.

Prayer:
"Lord, when anxiety creeps in, help me to turn to You for comfort. Fill my heart with Your peace and delight me with Your presence. Thank You for being my refuge. Amen."

Affirmation:
"I find comfort in God's presence, and His peace surrounds me even in times of anxiety."

Inspiration for the Day:
When anxious thoughts arise today, pause and seek God's comfort. Allow His peace to fill your heart and guide your thoughts.

a grateful Heart Sees Many blessings

www..queenbeetransformation.com

Reflection of the day

Day 6:

God is Your Shield

Scripture: 2 Samuel 22:31 (NIV)
"As for God, his way is perfect; the word of the Lord is tried: he is a buckler to all of them that trust in him."

Reflection:
God's ways are flawless, and His Word is trustworthy. He is our shield and protector, providing safety for those who place their trust in Him. Trusting in God means relying on His perfect plan for our lives, even when we can't see the entire picture.

Application:
Reflect on any areas of your life where you may feel uncertain or insecure. Surrender those concerns to God, trusting that His

plan is perfect and that He is protecting you.

1. **Trust in His Perfect Plan** – Even when life doesn't make sense, believe His way is best.
2. **Stand on His Word** – Fill your mind with scripture, knowing His promises never fail.
3. **Run to Him for Protection** – When storms hit, let God be your shield, not your own strength.

Prayer:
"Lord, I trust in Your perfect ways and Your promises. Help me to lean on You as my protector and guide in every aspect of my life. Thank You for being my stronghold. Amen."

Affirmation:
"I trust in God's perfect ways, and He is my shield and protector."

Inspiration for the Day:
Embrace God's perfect plan today. Trust Him to guide you through uncertainty and recognize His protection over your life.

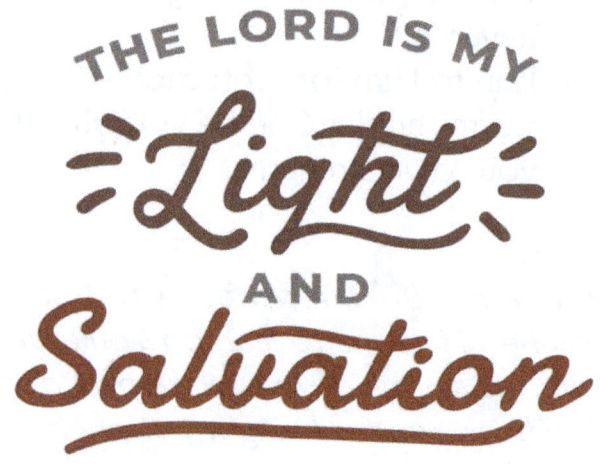

www..queenbeetransformation.com

Reflection of the day

Day 7:

Stand Firm in Faith

Scripture: 1 Peter 5:8-9 (NIV)
"Be sober, be vigilant; because your adversary the devil, as a roaring lion, walketh about, seeking whom he may devour: Whom resist stedfast in the faith, knowing that the same afflictions are accomplished in your brethren that are in the world."

Reflection:
We are in a spiritual battle, and being vigilant helps us recognize the enemy's tactics. However, we have the power to resist him through faith. Remembering that others face similar struggles can encourage us to stand firm in our beliefs and seek support from our community.

Application:
Strengthen your faith through prayer, scripture, and community support. Be proactive in resisting temptation and encouraging others in their faith.

1. **Stay Spiritually Alert** – The enemy looks for weak spots; stay prayed up and in God's Word.
2. **Fight Back with Faith** – When fear or doubt creep in, declare God's promises out loud.
3. **Stay Connected to the Body** – Surround yourself with strong believers who help you stand firm.

Prayer:
"Lord, help me to remain vigilant in my spiritual life. Strengthen my faith so that I can resist the enemy and encourage others to do the same. Thank You for Your protection. Amen."

Affirmation:
"I am vigilant in my faith, resisting the enemy and standing strong in God's promises."

Inspiration for the Day:

Stay alert today. Resist temptation with faith and support others in their struggles, knowing you're not alone in the fight.

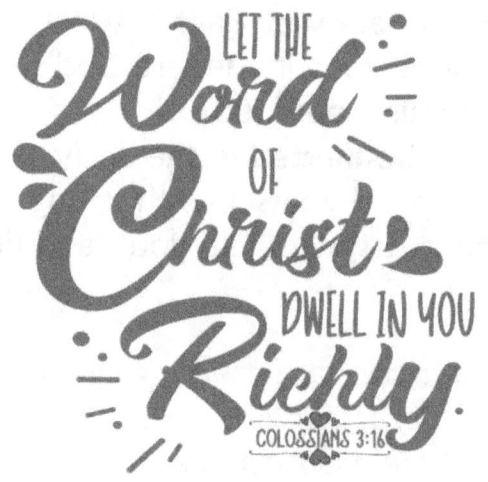

www..queenbeetransformation.com

Reflection of the day

Day 8:

God's Higher Ways

Scripture: Isaiah 55:8-9 (NIV)
"For my thoughts are not your thoughts, neither are your ways my ways," declares the Lord. "As the heavens are higher than the earth, so are my ways higher than your ways and my thoughts than your thoughts."

Reflection:
God's perspective far surpasses our own. When we face challenges, it's easy to become overwhelmed by our limited understanding. Trusting in His infinite wisdom helps us to navigate life's uncertainties with confidence, knowing He has a perfect plan.

Application:

When faced with confusion or difficulty today, remind yourself that God's thoughts and ways are higher than yours. Surrender your concerns to Him and ask for His guidance and understanding. Embrace the peace that comes from trusting His plan.

1. **Trust in His Plan** – Even when life feels uncertain, believe that God sees the bigger picture.
2. **Let Go of Control** – Surrender your plans to Him and embrace His perfect timing.
3. **Seek His Wisdom** – Instead of relying on your own understanding, pray for divine guidance.

Prayer:

"Lord, thank You for Your perfect wisdom. Help me to trust in Your ways, even when I don't understand. Guide me through my uncertainties and fill me with Your peace. Amen."

Affirmation:

"I trust in God's higher thoughts and ways, knowing He has a perfect plan for my life."

Inspiration for the Day:
When you encounter confusion or challenges today, remember that God sees the bigger picture. Trust Him and find comfort in His perfect plan.

www..queenbeetransformation.com

Reflection of the day

Day 9:

Love in Action

Scripture: Romans 12:10 (NIV)
"Be devoted to one another in love. Honor one another above yourselves."

Reflection:
Devotion and honor in relationships create a solid foundation for community and friendship. When we prioritize love and respect for others, we reflect the heart of God in our interactions.

Application:
Think of someone in your life who could benefit from your encouragement today. Reach out to them and show your appreciation or support. Look for ways to honor and serve those around you, putting

their needs above your own.

1. **Choose Kindness Daily** – Look for opportunities to uplift, serve, and show genuine love to others.
2. **Encourage and Honor Others** – Speak life into people and recognize their worth.
3. **Lead with Humility** – Put others before yourself, reflecting Christ's selfless love.

Prayer:
"Lord, help me with devotion to others in love and to honor them above myself. Teach me to see the value in those around me and to serve them selflessly. Amen."

Affirmation:
"I am devoted to love and honor others, reflecting the heart of God in my relationships."

Inspiration for the Day:
Today, find opportunities to show love and honor to those around you. A small act of kindness can make a big difference in someone's life.

www..queenbeetransformation.com

Reflection of the day

Day 10:

Never Alone

Scripture: Hebrews 13:5 (NIV)
"Keep your lives free from the love of money and be content with what you have, because God has said, 'Never will I leave you; never will I forsake you.'"

Reflection:
Contentment is a choice that requires us to focus on what we have rather than what we do not. This verse reassures us that God's presence in our lives is constant.

Application:
Take a moment to reflect on the blessings in Write down three things for which you are grateful. Shift your focus from what you desire to what you already possess and

embrace the contentment that comes from recognizing God's provision.

1. **Rest in His Presence** – No matter what you face, remind yourself that God is always with you.
2. **Let Go of Fear** – Stop worrying about abandonment or loneliness—He is your constant companion.
3. **Live with Confidence** – Walk boldly, knowing God's presence secures and strengthens you.

Prayer:
"Lord, help me to find contentment in my current situation. Thank You for Your unwavering presence in my life. I choose to focus on my blessings rather than my desires. Amen."

Affirmation:
"I am content in God's provision, trusting that He will never leave me or forsake me."

Inspiration for the Day:
Cultivate an attitude of gratitude today. Focus on the gifts you have, and let your heart be filled with contentment.

www..queenbeetransformation.com

Reflection of the day

Day 11:

Light for Your Path

Scripture: Psalm 119:105 (NIV)
"Your word is a lamp for my feet, a light on my path."

Reflection:
God's Word provides guidance and clarity in our lives. Like a lamp in the darkness, it illuminates our path, helping us to navigate through tough times. Trusting in His Word leads us to make wise decisions aligned with His will.

Application:
Spend time in God's Word today. Choose a passage to meditate on, allowing it to guide your thoughts and actions. Ask God for clarity in a specific area of your life where

you need direction. Journal Bible verses that stand out and speak to your life in the season you're in.

1. **Stay in the Word** – Let scripture be your daily guide in decision-making.
2. **Follow God's Leading** – When confused, turn to Him instead of the world's opinions.
3. **Take One Step at a Time** – God may not reveal everything at once but trust Him step by step.

Prayer:
"Lord, thank You for Your Word, which lights my path. Help me to seek Your guidance in every decision I make. Teach me to trust in Your direction, even when the way seems unclear. Amen."

Affirmation:
"God's Word guides me and lights my path, leading me toward His perfect will."

Inspiration for the Day:
Today, let God's Word illuminate your decisions and actions. Let his guidance and allow it to shape your journey.

www..queenbeetransformation.com

Reflection of the day

Day 12:

Wisdom from Above

Scripture: James 1:5 (NIV)
"If any of you lacks wisdom, you should ask God, who gives generously to all without finding fault, and it will be given to you."

Reflection:
God invites us to seek wisdom from Him, promising to provide it generously. No matter our circumstances or previous mistakes, He offers guidance without judgment.

Application:
Identify an area where you need wisdom. Take a moment to pray and ask God for His insight. Keep a journal to record the wisdom He provides and reflect on it

regularly. Practice recognizing daily knowledge in different scenarios.

1. **Ask for God's Guidance** – Pray daily for wisdom in your decisions and relationships.
2. **Listen and Apply** – Be open to His answers, even when they challenge you.
3. **Seek Wise Counsel** – Surround yourself with faith-filled mentors who encourage godly choices.

Prayer:
"Dear God, I come to You seeking wisdom. Thank You for Your promise to guide me generously. Help me to discern Your truth and apply it to my life. Amen."

Affirmation:
"I seek God's wisdom in every decision, knowing He generously provides guidance and insight."

Inspiration for the Day:
Today, approach decisions with an open heart, seeking God's wisdom. Trust that He will provide the clarity you need.

www.queenbeetransformation.com

Reflection of the day

Day 13:

Walk in Obedience

Scripture:
"Carefully follow the terms of this covenant, so that you may prosper in everything you do." – Deuteronomy 29:9 (NIV)

Reflection:
God's promises are unshakable, but they require our obedience. He doesn't ask for perfection—He asks for commitment, faith, and trust. When we align our lives with His Word, He positions us for blessings beyond what we can imagine. Prosperity isn't just financial; it's peace, favor, purpose, and strength in every season. God isn't holding anything back from you—He's leading you toward greater things. Your role? Stay faithful, stay grounded, and keep walking in obedience.

Application:
Today, evaluate where your heart and actions align with God's will. Are there areas where you've been hesitant to follow His lead? Maybe it's in your business, your relationships, or a personal struggle. Surrender those areas to Him. Take a bold step of faith today—whether it's making a decision based on His principles, speaking life over a situation, or trusting Him more fully with your future.

1. **Live by God's Standards** – Align your actions with His word, even when it's not popular.
2. **Stay Consistent** – Blessings come from daily faithfulness, not occasional obedience.
3. **Expect His Favor** – Trust that obedience leads to spiritual and practical prosperity.

Prayer:
Father, thank You for Your promises and the prosperity You have planned for me. Help me to walk in obedience, not out of fear, but out of love and trust in You. Give me discernment to follow Your path and

confidence to step into the blessings You've already set before me. I declare that I will prosper in every area of my life because I walk with You. In Jesus' name, Amen.

Affirmation:
I am obedient to God's Word, and He prospers me in every area of my life. My steps are ordered, my future is blessed, and I walk in divine favor.

Inspiration for the Day:
God's promises are like a blueprint for success. When you align with Him, you're not just surviving—you're thriving. Stay faithful, stay expectant, and watch how He moves in ways you never saw coming!

Reflection of the day

Day 14:

Power of Forgiveness

Scripture: Matthew 6:14-15 (NIV)
"For if you forgive other people when they sin against you, your heavenly Father will also forgive you. But if you do not forgive others their sins, your Father will not forgive your sins."

Reflection:
Holding onto grudges is like carrying a heavy burden, and forgiveness lifts that weight and sets us free. Jesus taught us to forgive so that we, too, may receive forgiveness from our Heavenly Father.

Application:
Reflect on Hurts: Take time to reflect on situations or people you need to forgive. Write down your feelings and thoughts.

1. **Let Go of Resentment** – Holding onto hurt only weighs you down; choose to release it.
2. **Forgive as You've Been Forgiven** – Remember that God extends grace to you daily.
3. **Pray for a Soft Heart** – Ask God to help you genuinely forgive, even when it's hard.

Prayer:
Dear God, I recognize the importance of forgiveness in my journey. Help me to let go of grudges and resentments, knowing that forgiveness is a gift I give to myself. Guide me in the path of healing and reconciliation, and may Your grace fill my heart. In Jesus' name, I pray. Amen.

Affirmation:
"I choose forgiveness as a pathway to healing and reconciliation. I let go of hurt and make space for God's grace to flow."

Inspiration for the Day:
Today, let forgiveness be an act of liberation. As you release grudges and resentment, you open the door to healing and restoration.

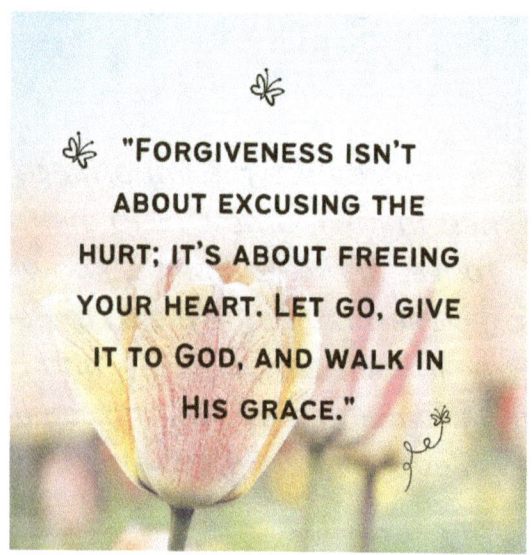

Reflection of the day

Day 15:

Give and Receive

Scripture:
"Give, and it will be given to you. A good measure, pressed down, shaken together and running over, will be poured into your lap. For with the measure you use, it will be measured to you." – Luke 6:38 (NIV)

Reflection:
God's Kingdom operates on a principle that the world can't understand: the more you give, the more you receive. This isn't just about money—it's about generosity in love, kindness, encouragement, and time. When you pour out from a willing and faithful heart, God ensures that what returns to you is overflowing. You can't out-give God. He sees your heart, your sacrifice, and your willingness to trust Him, and He responds

with abundance in ways you never expected.

Application:
Today, look for opportunities to give—whether it's your time, a kind word, a resource, or financial support. Don't give out of obligation but out of faith and joy. Trust that God sees every seed you plant and will return it to you in ways far beyond what you could imagine.

1. **Give Generously** – Give without hesitation, knowing God blesses a cheerful giver.
2. **Expect a Return** – Trust that what you give will come back to you in abundance.
3. **Live Open-Handed** – Be a channel of blessing, letting God use you to bless others.

Prayer:
Lord, thank You for being a generous God. Help me to have a heart like Yours—one that gives freely, trusts fully, and loves abundantly. I surrender my resources to You, knowing that You are my ultimate

provider. Let my generosity reflect Your love, and may I always be able to bless others. In Jesus' name, Amen.

Affirmation:
I am a cheerful giver, and God blesses me abundantly. As I pour out, He pours in, and my life overflows with favor and provision.

Inspiration for the Day:
When you give, you activate the principle of divine multiplication. Whether it's finances, kindness, or faith, God will return it to you in ways you never imagined. Give boldly and expect an overflow!

> "I AM A CHEERFUL GIVER, AND GOD BLESSES ME ABUNDANTLY—WHAT I POUR OUT, HE POURS BACK IN, OVERFLOWING MY LIFE WITH FAVOR AND PROVISION."

Reflection of the day

Day 16:

Soul Fully Satisfied

Scripture:
"My soul will be satisfied as with the richest of foods; with singing lips my mouth will praise you." – Psalm 63:5 (NIV)

Reflection:
True satisfaction isn't found in material things, achievements, or even relationships—it's found in God alone. When your soul is anchored in Him, you experience a joy and fulfillment that nothing else can provide. No matter what's happening around you, you can live in a state of peace, contentment, and praise because you know that God is more than enough.

Application:
Pause today and assess where you've been seeking satisfaction. Are you trying to fill an emptiness with temporary things? Shift your focus back to God. Spend intentional time in worship, prayer, or simply reflecting on His goodness.

1. **Seek God First** – Let Him be the source of your fulfillment.
2. **Savor Spiritual Nourishment** – Fill your heart with worship, scripture, and prayer.
3. **Praise Even in Lack** – Worship God not just for blessings, but for who He is.

Prayer:
Father, You alone satisfy my soul. No achievement, no possession, no earthly thing can compare to the joy of knowing You. Fill my heart with Your peace and remind me that I lack nothing in Your presence. Let my life be one of praise, no matter the circumstances. In Jesus' name, Amen.

Affirmation:
God is my source, and my soul is fully satisfied in Him. I live in peace, joy, and gratitude, knowing He is more than enough for me.

Inspiration for the Day:
Happiness fades, but true satisfaction lasts when it's rooted in God. Stop searching for fulfillment in temporary things—God is already offering you everything you need.

> "TRUE FULFILLMENT ISN'T FOUND IN TEMPORARY THINGS. PAUSE, REFOCUS, AND SEEK GOD—HIS PRESENCE IS THE ONLY THING THAT TRULY SATISFIES."

Reflection of the day

Day 17:

Blessings Without Sorrow

Scripture:
"The blessing of the Lord brings wealth, without painful toil for it." – Proverbs 10:22 (NIV)

Reflection:
God's blessings don't come with exhaustion, stress, or struggle. When He blesses you, it's different from what the world offers—His favor adds peace, not pressure. This doesn't mean you won't work hard, but it means your success will be built on His grace, not just your grind. When you align your work, goals, and efforts with His will, He brings opportunities, provision, and increase that you could never achieve on your own.

Application:
Instead of striving in your own strength, invite God into your work, your business, and your dreams. Ask Him to bless your efforts and guide your decisions. If you're feeling overwhelmed, take a step back and ensure that what you're pursuing is aligned with His purpose.

1. **Recognize God's Hand** – Every good thing in your life is a gift from Him.
2. **Let Go of Striving** – Stop chasing success and let God's blessings flow naturally.
3. **Enjoy the Blessing** – God's gifts come with joy, not stress—embrace them fully

Prayer:
Lord, I don't want to build my life on my own strength—I want to build it on Your blessing. Guide my steps, align my efforts with Your purpose, and open doors that only You can open. Thank You for bringing prosperity that is filled with peace, not pressure. I trust in Your plan. In Jesus' name, Amen.

Affirmation:
God's blessing brings success without stress. I am walking in divine favor, and my work is fruitful and prosperous.

Inspiration for the Day:
You don't have to hustle in exhaustion—when God's blessing is on your life, success comes with peace. Work hard, trust Him, and watch Him open doors effortlessly!

Reflection of the day

Day 18:

Prosper and Thrive

Scripture:
"Dear friend, I pray that you may enjoy good health and that all may go well with you, even as your soul is getting along well." – 3 John 1:2 (NIV)

Reflection:
God desires for you to be whole—spiritually, physically, and emotionally. His plan isn't for you to just get by; it's for you to thrive. But notice the order: as your soul prospers, everything else aligns. When your relationship with God is strong, it overflows into your health, your mindset, and your success.

Application:
Take a moment today to check in with

yourself. Are you prioritizing your spiritual growth? Are you taking care of your body and mind? Small daily choices—prayer, healthy habits, speaking life over yourself—will position you for the prosperity God intends for you.

1. **Speak Life Over Yourself** – Declare health, prosperity, and spiritual strength.
2. **Take Care of Your Body** – Steward your health as a gift from God.
3. **Align Your Goals with God** – Seek His wisdom in your financial, personal, and spiritual growth.

Prayer:
Father, I thank You that Your will for me is wholeness and prosperity in every area of my life. Guide me in making wise choices that align with the abundant life You have for me. In Jesus' name, Amen.

Affirmation:
My soul prospers, and so does every area of my life. I walk in health, favor, and divine alignment.

Inspiration for the Day:
God's blessings don't just touch one part of your life—they overflow into every aspect. Stay close to Him, and watch how He brings wholeness to your spirit, body, and future!

SELF-REMINDER

Waiting on God's timing is like waiting for your coffee to cool—impatiently blowing on it while knowing it's still too hot to handle!

www.queenbeetransformation.com

Reflection of the day

Day 19:

Honor Your Temple

Scripture:
"Do you not know that your bodies are temples of the Holy Spirit, who is in you, whom you have received from God? You are not your own; you were bought at a price. Therefore honor God with your bodies." – 1 Corinthians 6:19-20 (NIV)

Reflection:
Your body isn't just yours—it's a vessel for God's presence. That means how you treat it matters. Your energy, your health, your well-being all impact how effectively you can fulfill your purpose. Taking care of yourself isn't selfish; it's honoring the God who created you. When you see yourself as valuable, as God sees you, it changes the way you treat yourself.

Application:
Make one intentional decision today to care for your body—whether it's drinking more water, exercising, getting rest, or fueling yourself with healthy food.

1. **Make Healthy Choices** – Nourish your body with good food, rest, and exercise.
2. **Guard Your Heart & Mind** – Protect yourself from toxic influences.
3. **Dedicate Your Body to God** – Use your body to honor Him in all you do.

Prayer:
Lord, thank You for creating me in Your image and filling me with Your Spirit. Help me to honor You by taking care of my body, mind, and spirit. Give me wisdom and discipline to make choices that reflect the value You have placed on me. In Jesus' name, Amen.

Affirmation:
My body is a temple of the Holy Spirit, and I treat it with care and respect. I am strong, valuable, and created for a purpose.

Inspiration for the Day:
Taking care of yourself isn't just about looking good—it's about being strong enough to step fully into your calling. You are worth the investment!

"May every sip remind you that grace is poured out freely — for healing, for hope, and for the beautiful journey ahead."

www.queenbeetransformation.com

Reflection of the day

Day 20:

God Grants Desires

Scripture:
"May He give you the desire of your heart and make all your plans succeed." – Psalm 20:4 (NIV)

Reflection:
God cares about your dreams. He isn't just watching from a distance—He's actively working behind the scenes to align your desires with His perfect will. When your heart seeks Him first, your plans aren't just your own; they become divinely guided steps toward success. Trust that He sees your efforts, your faith, and your obedience, and He is bringing everything together in His perfect timing.

Application:
Write down one dream or goal you've been praying about. Surrender it fully to God, trusting that He will bring it to pass in the right way and at the right time.

1. **Align Your Desires with God** – Seek His will first in all your plans.
2. **Pray with Expectancy** – Ask God for the desires of your heart and trust Him to answer.
3. **Take Inspired Action** – Move forward in faith as if your prayers are already answered.

Prayer:
Father, thank You for planting dreams in my heart. I trust that You are guiding my steps and aligning my desires with Your perfect plan. Help me to stay faithful and take action, knowing that success comes from You. In Jesus' name, Amen.

Affirmation:
God is making my dreams a reality. My plans succeed because they are aligned with His purpose.

Inspiration for the Day:
If God put it in your heart, He will bring it to life. Stay faithful, stay expectant, and watch Him move!

"Gratitude turns what we have into enough and opens our hearts to the endless grace God pours into our lives."

www.queenbeetransformation.com

Reflection of the day

Day 21:

Delight and Trust

Scripture:
"Take delight in the Lord, and He will give you the desires of your heart. Commit your way to the Lord; trust in Him and He will do this." – Psalm 37:4-5 (NIV)

Reflection:
Delighting in the Lord isn't just about asking for blessings—it's about falling in love with Him. When you seek God first, He reshapes your desires to align with His best for you. Sometimes we chase things that we think will fulfill us, but God has something even greater in store. Trust Him, surrender your plans, and watch how He brings everything together beautifully.

Application:
Instead of stressing over what you want to happen, shift your focus to simply seeking God. Spend time in worship, prayer, and gratitude. As you do, He will refine your desires and lead you to exactly where you're meant to be.

1. **Make God Your Priority** – Find joy in spending time with Him daily.
2. **Surrender Control** – Hand your plans over to God and trust Him to guide you.
3. **Watch Him Work** – Stay patient and watch how He unfolds your journey.

Prayer:
Lord, I surrender my plans to You. Help me to delight in You above all else and trust that You know what's best for me. Align my heart with Your will and lead me into the blessings You have prepared. In Jesus' name, Amen.

Affirmation:
I delight in the Lord, and He aligns my desires with His perfect plan. My steps are ordered, and my future is secure.

Inspiration for the Day:
When you chase after God, blessings chase after you. Stay close to Him, and watch your dreams unfold!

"When you trust God's guidance, every step forward —no matter how small—leads to a life rebuilt in grace and purpose."

www.queenbeetransformation.com

Reflection of the day

Day 22:

Confidence Brings Reward

Scripture:
"So do not throw away your confidence; it will be richly rewarded." – Hebrews 10:35 (NIV)

Reflection:
Confidence isn't arrogance—it's trust in who God says you are and what He has promised you. The enemy will try to shake your faith, whispering doubts, delays, and distractions. But don't let go of your confidence. God is faithful, and if He said it, He will do it. The reward is coming—keep pressing forward with boldness!

Application:
Speak life over yourself today. Declare God's promises with confidence. If you've

been feeling discouraged, remind yourself of past victories and God's faithfulness. Stand firm, knowing that your confidence in Him will bring the breakthrough you've been waiting for.

1. **Hold on to Faith** – No matter what, don't let go of your confidence in God.
2. **Declare Victory Daily** – Speak God's promises over your life with confidence.
3. **Trust in God's Timing** – Your reward is coming—don't give up too soon!

Prayer:
Father, thank You for being a faithful God. Strengthen my confidence in Your promises, and help me to stand firm in faith, no matter what I see. I trust that You are working behind the scenes, and I refuse to let doubt steal my expectation. In Jesus' name, Amen.

Affirmation:
I am confident in God's promises, and I refuse to give up. My breakthrough is coming, and I am richly rewarded.

Inspiration for the Day:
Don't let fear steal what faith has secured. Stay confident, keep believing, and watch God show up in ways you never expected!

"God's love is the constant light that leads you through the darkest valleys, reminding you that you are seen, chosen, and never alone."

www.queenbeetransformation.com

Reflection of the day

Day 23:

Write the Vision

Scripture:
"Then the Lord replied: 'Write down the revelation and make it plain on tablets so that a herald may run with it. For the revelation awaits an appointed time; it speaks of the end and will not prove false. Though it lingers, wait for it; it will certainly come and will not delay.'" – Habakkuk 2:2-3 (NIV)

Reflection:
God is a God of vision and purpose. When He places a dream or calling in your heart, it is for an appointed time. Delays don't mean denial! He tells us to write it down, make it plain, and stay the course. Just because you don't see it happening yet

doesn't mean it's not on the way. Trust in His perfect timing.

Application:
If you haven't already, write down the vision God has given you. Keep it where you can see it daily as a reminder of His promises. Take small, consistent steps toward it and trust that He is working behind the scenes to bring it to pass.

1. **Write It Down** – Get clear on your vision and write it in detail.
2. **Stay Patient** – Trust God's timing, even when things seem slow.
3. **Keep the Faith** – Keep believing in your vision, even when doubts arise.

Prayer:
Lord, thank You for the dreams and vision You've placed in my heart. Give me patience and perseverance to wait on Your perfect timing. Help me to stay focused and faithful, knowing that what You have spoken will come to pass. In Jesus' name, Amen.

Affirmation:
God's vision for my life is unfolding in perfect timing. I am patient, faithful, and expectant.

Inspiration for the Day:
A delayed promise is not a denied promise. Keep believing, keep preparing, and watch God move!

HOPE

blooms in the heart that trusts God's love — unwavering, unending, and always working for your good."

www.queenbeetransformation.com

Reflection of the day

Day 24:

Grace is Enough

Scripture:
"But He said to me, 'My grace is sufficient for you, for My power is made perfect in weakness.' Therefore I will boast all the more gladly about my weaknesses, so that Christ's power may rest on me." – 2 Corinthians 12:9 (NIV)

Reflection:
You don't have to be strong all the time. In fact, it's in your weakness that God's strength shines the most. When you feel like you can't go on, His grace carries you. When you feel unqualified, He equips you. Lean into His grace—it's more than enough.

Application:
Instead of trying to do everything in your

own strength, surrender to God's power. The next time you feel weak, stop and remind yourself: *God's got this. I don't have to carry it alone.*

1. **Let Go of Perfection** – God's grace covers your weaknesses—stop striving for flawlessness.
2. **Rely on Him** – When you feel weak, turn to God instead of pushing through alone.
3. **Celebrate His Strength** – Shift your focus from what you lack to what God provides.

Prayer:
Lord, I thank You that Your grace is enough for me. When I am weak, You are strong. Help me to rely on Your strength instead of my own. Fill me with peace, knowing that You are carrying me through every challenge. In Jesus' name, Amen.

Affirmation:
God's grace is sufficient for me. In my weakness, His strength is revealed.

Inspiration for the Day:
You don't have to be strong all the time—just be surrendered. Let God's power work through you!

"True peace is found when you surrender your worries to God, knowing His love holds every piece of your story."

www.queenbeetransformation.com

Reflection of the day

Day 25:

Run with Endurance

Scripture:
"Therefore, since we are surrounded by such a great cloud of witnesses, let us throw off everything that hinders and the sin that so easily entangles. And let us run with perseverance the race marked out for us." – Hebrews 12:1 (NIV)

Reflection:
Life is a race, but it's not about speed—it's about endurance. The enemy loves to weigh us down with distractions, doubts, and fear. But God calls us to *throw off* those things and keep our eyes on the finish line. You are not running alone; heaven is cheering you on!

Application:
Identify what's slowing you down—fear, doubt, comparison, bad habits—and make a conscious decision to let it go. Focus on your race, not anyone else's.

1. **Release the Weight** – Let go of past regrets, guilt, or distractions that slow you down.
2. **Stay Focused on Jesus** – Keep your eyes on Him rather than comparing your race to others.
3. **Build Consistency** – Faith is a marathon, not a sprint—take daily steps forward.

Prayer:
Lord, help me to run my race with endurance. Show me what I need to release so I can move forward freely. Strengthen me when I feel weary and remind me that I am never running alone. In Jesus' name, Amen.

Affirmation:
I run my race with perseverance. Nothing holds me back from my God-given purpose.

Inspiration for the Day:
Don't look at the runners beside you—stay focused on your lane. God has already marked your path!

"In every sunrise and blooming flower, God reveals His promise — a masterpiece in motion, reminding you that His creation includes you.

www.queenbeetransformation.com

Reflection of the day

Day 26:

Be Strong, Stand

Scripture:
"Finally, be strong in the Lord and in His mighty power." – Ephesians 6:10 (NIV)

Reflection:
Strength isn't about how much you can handle—it's about how much you trust God to handle for you. His power is limitless, and when you lean on Him, you walk in supernatural strength. No battle is too big when you stand in His power.

Application:
Start your day by declaring strength over your life. Whenever you feel overwhelmed, stop and remind yourself: *God is my source of strength—I don't have to do this alone.*

1. **Start Your Day in Prayer** – Ask for strength before facing challenges.
2. **Put on Spiritual Armor** – Stand firm in truth, faith, and God's promises.
3. **Declare Victory** – Speak strength over your life with scripture-based affirmations.

Prayer:
Lord, I choose to stand in Your strength, not my own. Fill me with Your power and courage to face whatever comes my way. I trust that You are fighting for me. In Jesus' name, Amen.

Affirmation:
I am strong in the Lord. His power works in me and through me.

Inspiration for the Day:
You don't need to be the strongest—just be the most surrendered. His power will carry you!

SHARE
THE
JOY

www.queenbeetransformation.com

Reflection of the day

Day 27:

Honor and Overflow

Scripture:
"Honor the Lord with your wealth, with the firstfruits of all your crops; then your barns will be filled to overflowing, and your vats will brim over with new wine." – Proverbs 3:9-10 (NIV)

Reflection:
When you put God first in your finances, time, and resources, He blesses you abundantly. It's not about what you lose—it's about what He multiplies. Honoring God invites overflow into your life.

Application:
Give God your *first*, not your leftovers. Whether it's your finances, time, or talents,

trust that He will provide more than enough.

1. **Give God First Place** – Prioritize Him in your time, finances, and decisions.
2. **Be a Generous Giver** – Honor God by giving freely without fear.
3. **Expect Overflow** – Trust that God will always provide more than enough.

Prayer:
Lord, I choose to honor You with all that I have. Teach me to be generous, faithful, and trust in Your provision. I believe that as I give, You will bless me abundantly. In Jesus' name, Amen.

Affirmation:
I honor God with my resources, and He blesses me beyond measure.

Inspiration for the Day:
God's math is different—when you give, He multiplies. Trust Him first and watch Him overflow your life!

www.queenbeetransformation.com

Reflection of the day

Day 28:

Believe it's Possible

Scripture:
"'If you can'?" said Jesus. 'Everything is possible for one who believes.'" – Mark 9:23 (NIV)

Reflection:
Faith unlocks the impossible. If you're doubting, shift your mindset. Jesus didn't say *some* things are possible—He said *everything*. What are you believing for? God is bigger than your situation!

Application:
Speak faith over your circumstances. Instead of saying *if*, start saying *when*. Believe that God is moving, even when you don't see it yet.

1. **Eliminate Doubt** – Speak faith, not fear, over your dreams.
2. **Pray Boldly** – Bring big prayers before God, believing in His power.
3. **Take Action** – Step out in faith and act like your miracle is already on its way.

Prayer:
Lord, I believe that nothing is impossible with You. Strengthen my faith and help me to trust You completely. I declare breakthroughs and miracles in Jesus' name, Amen.

Affirmation:
Everything is possible for me because I believe.

Inspiration for the Day:
If God said *everything is possible*, why limit yourself? Dream bigger!

Step out of your comfort ZONE.

www.queenbeetransformation.com

Reflection of the day

Day 29:

Release the Burden

Scripture:
"Cast your cares on the Lord and He will sustain you; He will never let the righteous be shaken." – Psalm 55:22 (NIV)

Reflection:
God never intended for you to carry the weight of the world on your shoulders. Whatever is troubling your heart today, He is ready to take it. When you release your burdens to Him, He replaces them with His peace and strength. You don't have to be shaken by life's storms—God is holding you steady.

Application:
Make it a habit to *cast* your cares instead of carrying them. When worry creeps in, take

a deep breath and pray: *Lord, I give this to You.* Release it and trust that He will sustain you.

1. **Pray & Surrender** – Start your day by giving your worries to God in prayer.
2. **Replace Worry with Faith** – When anxiety creeps in, replace it with scripture and affirmations.
3. **Take One Step** – Trust that God will sustain you and focus on just the next right step.

Prayer:
Father, I lay down my burdens before You. I trust that You will sustain me and hold me firm in Your hands. Help me to remember that I don't have to carry these worries alone. In Jesus' name, Amen.

Affirmation:
I cast my cares on the Lord, and He strengthens and sustains me.

Inspiration for the Day:
God never asked you to carry it all—He asked you to *cast it on Him.* Let it go, and let God work!

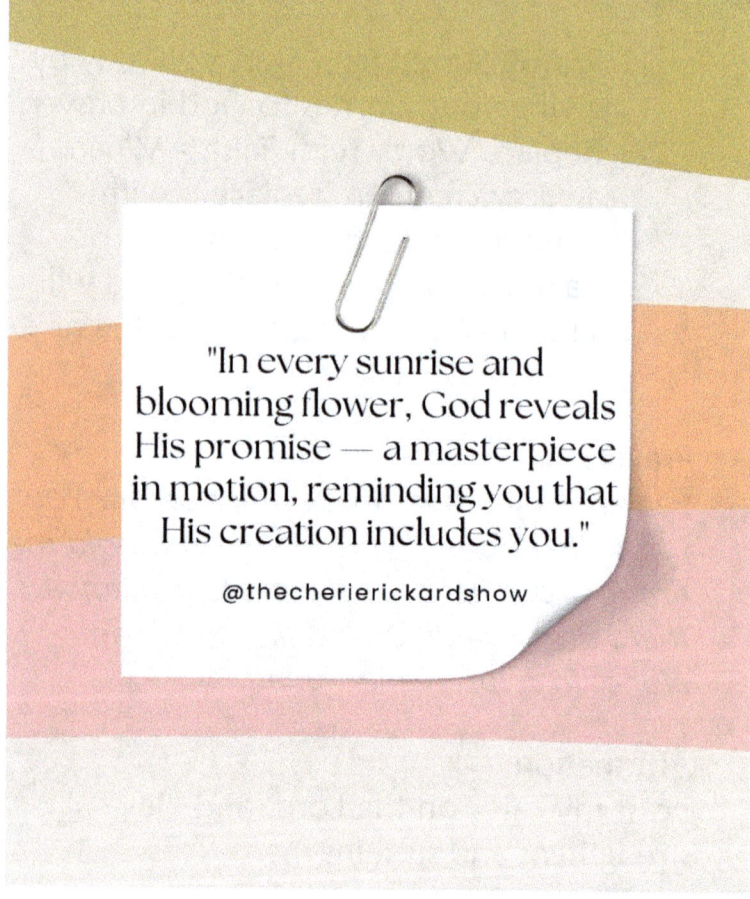

Reflection of the day

Day 30:

God Sees You

Scripture:
"But the eyes of the Lord are on those who fear Him, on those whose hope is in His unfailing love." – Psalm 33:18 (NIV)

Reflection:
You are seen. You are known. You are loved. God's eyes are always on you—not to condemn, but to guide, protect, and cover you with His love. When your hope is in Him, you are never alone, never forgotten, and never without direction.

Application:
Shift your focus from the problem to the One who is watching over you. Keep your hope anchored in His love, and trust that

He is leading you exactly where you need to be.

1. **Rest in His Love** – Remind yourself daily that God watches over you with love, not judgment.
2. **Shift Your Focus** – Instead of worrying about the unknown, trust that His eyes are guiding you.
3. **Speak Life Over Yourself** – Declare, *God sees me, loves me, and has good plans for me.*

Prayer:
Lord, thank You for watching over me and keeping me in Your care. I place my hope in You, knowing that Your love never fails. Help me to trust You completely. In Jesus' name, Amen.

Affirmation:
God sees me, loves me, and leads me. My hope is in Him.

Inspiration for the Day:
If God's eyes are always on you, why worry? Rest in His love—He's got you covered.

www.queenbeetransformation.com

Reflection of the day

I am sorry for what I said before I had my coffee with Christ ♡

Setting Boundaries with Grace and Living with Purpose.

Whether you're navigating grief, betrayal, or simply trying to rediscover your own voice, this episode is for you.

I want to remind you – setting boundaries isn't about shutting people out or being selfish. It's about creating space for God's purpose to thrive in your life. Boundaries are a form of self-respect and a way of aligning your life with what God has called you to do.

Why Boundaries Matter in Your Healing Journey: After adversity, it's easy to feel like you're at the mercy of everyone else's needs and opinions. But God never intended for us to live depleted or stretched beyond what we were created to bear.

Proverbs 4:23 says, *"Above all else, guard your heart, for everything you do flows from it."*

Guarding your heart starts with setting boundaries. When you protect your peace, you're protecting the life God is rebuilding within you.

Real-Life Situations: Let's talk about what setting boundaries looks like in everyday life:

- Maybe you've always said *yes* to every request from family and friends because you didn't want to disappoint anyone – but now you're left feeling drained.
- Or maybe you've allowed toxic relationships to linger because you're afraid of confrontation.
- Perhaps you're pouring all your time into work or others, leaving no room to nurture your relationship with God or pursue the dreams He's placed in your heart.

I've been there. After losing my son and walking through some of the hardest moments of my life, I had to learn the hard way that boundaries aren't just necessary – they're *holy*. They're part of the rebuilding process God leads us through.

Setting Boundaries with Grace: Boundaries aren't about cutting people off – they're about creating healthy expectations rooted in love. Here's how you can set boundaries with grace:

1. **Pray First:** Before making any decision, bring it to God. Ask Him for wisdom and clarity.
    - Scripture: *"If any of you lacks wisdom, let him ask of God, who gives to all liberally and without reproach, and it will be given to him."* – James 1:5
2. **Define What You Need:** Be specific about what needs to change. Is it more time for yourself? Space from a draining relationship? Time to pursue your calling?
    - Journal Prompt: What areas of my life feel out of balance right now?
3. **Communicate with Kindness:** Speak your truth in love. You can say, *"I care about you, but I need to prioritize my own healing right now."*
    - Scripture: *"Let your conversation be always full of grace, seasoned with salt, so that you may know how to answer everyone."* – Colossians 4:6
4. **Stand Firm Without Guilt:** People may not always like your boundaries, but you're not responsible for their reactions

– you're responsible for your obedience to God.
  - Affirmation: *"I am worthy of protecting my peace and living in alignment with God's purpose."*

Living with Purpose: Once you've created space through boundaries, the next step is filling that space with God's purpose for your life.

Your pain doesn't disqualify you – it *positions* you. Every setback, betrayal, or broken moment is part of the testimony God is writing through you.

Jeremiah 29:11 reminds us, *"For I know the plans I have for you," declares the Lord, "plans to prosper you and not to harm you, plans to give you hope and a future."*

Action Steps to Live with Purpose:

1. Spend time in prayer each morning asking God to reveal His plan for your day.
2. Identify one small step you can take each day toward your vision – whether it's

starting that book, signing up for a class, or making time to rest and restore.
3. Surround yourself with a supportive community – people who remind you who you are in Christ.

Closing Prayer: Lord, thank You for the strength to rebuild and the wisdom to set boundaries that align with Your purpose. Help me to guard my heart, protect my peace, and step boldly into the life You are calling me to. Let my life reflect Your grace and goodness. In Jesus' name, Amen.

If this devotional spoke to you, share it with a friend or sister who needs the love of Christ. And if you're ready to go deeper, join our Queen Bee Transformation community where we rebuild, rise, and thrive together. Go to www.queenbeetransformation.com

Remember – setting boundaries is not selfish. It's an act of obedience. You are worthy of a life filled with purpose, peace, and grace. Until next time, keep rising, keep shining, and keep walking in faith.

Grief & Adversity – More Than Just Loss

Grief isn't just about losing a loved one—it's about losing anything you once held dear. Whether it's the end of a relationship, a betrayal, a lost dream, or an identity shaken by life's unexpected turns, grief shows up in many forms. In this episode, we're breaking the myth that grief is only tied to death and diving into the ways loss and adversity shape us.

If you've ever felt broken by loss, shaken by change, or wounded by life, this conversation is for you. We'll explore how to navigate grief, find purpose in pain, and move forward without losing yourself. Healing is possible, and you don't have to do it alone.

✨ If you're looking for daily encouragement, grab one of my devotionals to find strength and inspiration. If you're ready for true transformation, **Queen Bee Transformation** is here to help you rise stronger than ever. Let's heal and grow together!

ABOUT THE AUTHOR

Meet Cherie Rickard, a healthcare professional, dedicated Christian motivational speaker, and an expert in navigating life's adversities. With an unwavering commitment to spreading hope and empowerment, Cherie has become a beacon of inspiration for countless individuals seeking to overcome challenges and embrace the power of faith.

Cherie brings a unique perspective to her writing, infusing her words with compassion, understanding, and a deep appreciation for life's journey. As a Christian motivational speaker, she has captivated audiences delivering soul-stirring messages of resilience, faith, and transformation.

Beyond her impactful speaking engagements, Cherie is the driving force behind the widely acclaimed podcast "The Cherie Rickard Show" Through candid conversations and authentic storytelling, she dives into real-life experiences, offering listeners a safe space to explore vulnerability, personal growth, and the triumph of the human spirit.

Cherie's remarkable journey is a testament to her own triumph over adversity, making her an authentic guide for those seeking to find strength during life's trials.

Whether through her powerful talks, her engaging podcast, or her insightful written works, Cherie continues to touch hearts and inspire transformation.

Join her on a journey of faith, resilience, and the boundless potential that lies within each one of us.

Please Join Me For

Coffee & Blessings

**The Cherie Rickard Show
Tune in Each Week!**

ANYWHERE PODCAST ARE HEARD

Discover more about Cherie's work, passion, and profound impact as you immerse yourself in the pages *Coffee with Christ, Brewed Blessings* and *Cup of Grace!*

Follow her on social media [@thecherierickardshow](#), and tune in every week to [The Cherie Rickard Show](#)

Do you ever feel like you are stuck in your story, ready for a new chapter but not sure where to begin? After life's toughest challenges, whether it's grief, a tough breakup, betrayal, or just feeling lost, it's easy to feel unsure about your next step. That's where my one-on-one coaching program comes in!

[Queen Bee Transformation](#)

www.ingramcontent.com/pod-product-compliance
Lightning Source LLC
LaVergne TN
LVHW021117080426
835512LV00011B/2551